Pooh's Little Etiquette Book

Pooh's Little Etiquette Book

INSPIRED BY *A. A. Milne*

DECORATIONS BY *Ernest H. Shepard*

DUTTON BOOKS · NEW YORK

Published in the United States 1995 by Dutton Children's Books,
a division of Penguin Books USA Inc.
375 Hudson Street, New York, New York 10014
Written by Melissa Dorfman France
Designed by Adrian Leichter
Printed in Mexico
ISBN 0-525-45501-9
FIRST EDITION
6 8 10 9 7 5

❧ *Contents* ❧

❧ Introduction ❧

"Well," said Owl, "the customary procedure in such cases is as follows."

"What does Crustimoney Proseedcake mean?" said Pooh. "For I am a Bear of Very Little Brain, and long words Bother me."

"It means the Thing to Do." *Winnie-the-Pooh*

E*ven in a place as welcoming and friendly as the Hundred Acre Wood, there is a right way and a wrong way to behave in a social setting. And even for those with a Great Deal of Brain, it is sometimes difficult to know the correct Thing to Do.*

So here is a Very Useful Book that provides advice on Proper Comportment in a wide range of situations. As Pooh and his friends helpfully demonstrate how (and how not) to visit and entertain, eat, correspond, and make conversation, Clever Readers will learn much about making the Social Round.

Whether or not they are already acquainted with the rules of etiquette, readers will find that knowing the finer points of life in the Hundred Acre Wood will also serve them well in the world beyond, making this a book that is, as Christopher Robin would say, a comforting sort of thing to have.

Visiting

—✺—

Dropping in unannounced to pay a social call is perfectly acceptable in the Hundred Acre Wood. However, keep in mind that the friend you want to visit may or may not admit to being at home.

—✺—

Pooh bent down, put his head into the hole, and called out: "Is anybody at home?"

There was a sudden scuffling noise from inside the hole, and then silence.

"What I said was, 'Is anybody at home?'" called out Pooh very loudly.

"No!" said a voice; and then added, "you needn't shout so loud. I heard you quite well the first time." *Winnie-the-Pooh*

If you feel awkward visiting friends without a special Reason, tell them you've come to wish them a Very Happy Thursday.

―❈―

Unexpected guests should not ask their host for tea—even if it is Time-for-a-little-something. A very subtle hint, however (such as a wistful look toward the cupboard), is allowable.

―❈―

"Hallo, Owl," said Pooh. "I hope we're not too late for—
I mean, how are you, Owl? Piglet and I just came to see how
you were, because it's Thursday."

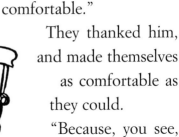

"Sit down, Pooh, sit down, Piglet," said
Owl kindly. "Make yourselves
comfortable."

They thanked him,
and made themselves
as comfortable as
they could.

"Because, you see,
Owl," said Pooh,
"we've been hurrying,

so as to be in time for—so as to see you before we went away
again."   *The House At Pooh Corner*

15

When offered a meal, the polite visitor shows appreciation for whatever the host is serving. If the visitor's enthusiasm is genuine, this is even better.

Pooh always liked a little something at eleven o'clock in the morning, and he was very glad to see Rabbit getting out the plates and mugs; and when Rabbit said, "Honey or condensed milk with your bread?" he was so excited that he said, "Both."

Winnie-the-Pooh

*W*hen you want to end a visit early, it is tactful to give a reason for leaving, so as not to hurt your host's feelings. A believable reason is best.

"I have just remembered something that I forgot to do yester-day and shan't be able to do tomorrow."

"We'll do it this afternoon, and I'll come with you," said Pooh.

"It isn't the sort of thing you can do in the afternoon," said Piglet quickly. "It's a very particular morning thing, that has to be done in the morning, and, if possible, between the hours of—— What would you say the time was?"

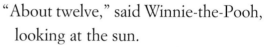

"About twelve," said Winnie-the-Pooh, looking at the sun.

"Between, as I was say-ing, the hours of twelve and twelve five. So, really, dear old Pooh, if you'll excuse me——"

Winnie-the-Pooh

———⟨∞⟩———

Be sure to thank your host politely before you leave, and write a thank-you note soon after. This is not only good etiquette but a good way to let your friend know that you arrived home safely.

———⟨∞⟩———

"I expect he's just gone home," said Christopher Robin to Rabbit.

"Did he say Good-bye-and-thank-you-for-a-nice-time?" said Rabbit.

"He'd only just said how-do-you-do," said Christopher Robin.

"Ha!" said Rabbit. "Has he written a letter saying how much he enjoyed himself, and how sorry he was he had to go so suddenly?"

Christopher Robin didn't think he had.

"Ha!" said Rabbit again, and looked very important. "This is Serious."

The House At Pooh Corner

Table Manners

When it is time to eat, be careful where you sit down. What is a Resting Place to you may be Lunch to someone else.

Eeyore looked round at them in his melancholy way. "I suppose none of you are sitting on a thistle by any chance?"

"I believe I am," said Pooh. "Ow!" He got up, and looked behind him. "Yes, I was. I thought so."

"Thank you, Pooh. If you've quite finished with it." He moved across to Pooh's place, and began to eat.

"It don't do them any Good, you know, sitting on them," he went on, as he looked up munching. "Takes all the Life out of them."

Winnie-the-Pooh

If you cannot find a seat at the table, sit with your friends-and-relations on the grass nearby. If you wait hopefully, somebody may drop something.

Don't rearrange your host's table setting, even if you think that it is trying to bite you.

Tigger said: "Excuse me a moment, but there's something climbing up your table," and with one loud *Worraworraworraworraworra* he jumped at the end of the tablecloth, pulled it to the ground, wrapped himself up in it three times, rolled to the other end of the room, and, after a terrible struggle, got his head into the daylight again, and said cheerfully: "Have I won?"

The House At Pooh Corner

When your host serves an unfamiliar dish,
try it with an open mind. You may find that this is the
food you like best. (Then again, you may not.)

Pooh put a large honey-pot on the cloth, and they sat down to breakfast. And as soon as they sat down, Tigger took a large mouthful of honey…and he looked up at the ceiling with his head on one side, and made exploring noises with his tongue and considering noises, and what-have-we-got-*here* noises…and then he said in a very decided voice:

"Tiggers don't like honey."   *The House At Pooh Corner*

It is poor etiquette to gulp down someone else's Strengthening Medicine—unless, of course, they don't like it themselves.

———— ⬦ ————

It is also impolite—and often messy—to speak with your mouth full.

———— ⬦ ————

Kanga said to Roo, "Drink up your milk first, dear, and talk afterwards." So Roo, who was drinking his milk, tried to say that he could do both at once...and had to be patted on the back and dried for quite a long time afterwards. *Winnie-the-Pooh*

———— ⋙≡⋘ ————

Eating heartily is a compliment to the cook.
But try not to appear more interested in the meal than
in the friend with whom you are sharing it.

———— ⋙≡⋘ ————

When Rabbit said, "Honey or condensed milk with your bread?" Pooh was so excited that he said, "Both," and then, so as not to seem greedy, he added, "but don't bother about the bread, please." And for a long time after that he said nothing...until at last, humming to himself in a rather sticky voice, he got up, shook Rabbit lovingly by the paw, and said that he must be going on.

Winnie-the-Pooh

And avoid eating so heartily that you cannot
fit through the door when the meal is over.

"The fact is," said Rabbit, "you're stuck."

"It all comes," said Pooh crossly, "of not having front doors big enough."

"It all comes," said Rabbit sternly, "of eating too much. I thought at the time," said Rabbit, "only I didn't like to say anything," said Rabbit, "that one of us was eating too much," said Rabbit, "and I knew it wasn't *me*."

Winnie-the-Pooh

Entertaining

If you enjoy having visitors, you can
make your home more inviting by installing both
a knocker and a bell-pull.

⊗⊗⊗

But be sure to put the knocker fairly low on your door,
in case a Very Small friend drops by.

⊗⊗⊗

"Hallo, Pooh," said Piglet.

"What are *you* trying to do?"

"I was trying to reach the knocker," said Piglet. "I just came round——"

"Let me do it for you," said Pooh kindly. So he reached up and knocked at the door.

"But Pooh," said Piglet, "it's your own house!"

"Oh!" said Pooh. "So it is," he said. "Well, let's go in."

Winnie-the-Pooh

When unexpected guests show up in the evening, it is gracious to offer them a meal and a place to sleep. It is not necessary to give them your bed, however, especially if their visit got you up out of it.

"Well," said Pooh, "it's the middle of the night, which is a good time for going to sleep. And tomorrow morning we'll have some honey for breakfast. Do Tiggers like honey?"

"They like everything," said Tigger cheerfully.

"Then if they like going to sleep on the floor, I'll go back to bed," said Pooh.   *The House At Pooh Corner*

*It is perfectly appropriate to politely ask a
guest who is spending several days in your home to lend
a hand (or paw) around the house.*

"We'll read to you," said Rabbit cheerfully. "And I hope it won't snow," he added. "And I say, old fellow, you're taking up a good deal of room in my house—*do* you mind if I use your back legs as a towel-horse? Because, I mean, there they are—doing nothing—and it would be very convenient just to hang the towels on them."

Winnie-the-Pooh

A good host offers his guests the tastiest food he has, even if he has been saving it for another occasion.

Eeyore led the way to the most thistly-looking patch of thistles that ever was, and waved a hoof at it.

"A little patch I was keeping for my birthday," he said; "but, after all, what are birthdays? Here today and gone tomorrow. Help yourself, Tigger." *The House At Pooh Corner*

---⚬⚬⚬---

If a guest should turn down your favorite food,
try to sound Sad and Regretful.

---⚬⚬⚬---

If you are not sure what your guests want to eat,
it is thoughtful simply to let them help themselves.

---⚬⚬⚬---

Kanga said very kindly, "Well, look in my cupboard, Tigger dear, and see what you'd like."

"Shall I look, too?" said Pooh, who was beginning to feel a little eleven o'clockish. And he found a small tin of condensed milk, and something seemed to tell him that Tiggers didn't like this, so he took it into a corner by itself, and went with it to see that nobody interrupted it. *The House At Pooh Corner*

*Near the end of a meal, it is polite to ask
your guests if they would like a little more. But it is
a good idea to check first to see if there is
any more to give them.*

———— ⬿ ————

*When your guests prepare to leave, act sorry
to see them go. But if it seems as though they may never
leave, a subtle nudge is appropriate.*

———— ⬿ ————

At last, humming to himself in a rather sticky voice, Pooh got up, shook Rabbit lovingly by the paw, and said that he must be going on.

"Must you?" said Rabbit politely.

"Well," said Pooh, "I could stay a little longer if it—if you——" and he tried very hard to look in the direction of the larder.

"As a matter of fact," said Rabbit, "I was going out myself directly."

Winnie-the-Pooh

A good host will make guests feel glad they visited and eager to come again.

"When you suddenly go into somebody's house, and he says, 'Hallo, Pooh, you're just in time for a little smackerel of something,' and you are, then it's what I call a Friendly Day."

The House At Pooh Corner

❧ Conversation ❧

Upon bumping into friends or acquaintances, it is courteous to ask how they are. However, you should sincerely want to hear the answer.

"And how are you?" said Winnie-the-Pooh.

Eeyore shook his head from side to side.

"Not very how," he said. "I don't seem to have felt at all how for a long time."

Winnie-the-Pooh

Weather is a good topic with which to start
a conversation, as the weather, good or bad, is of
interest to almost everyone.

"It's snowing still," said Eeyore gloomily.

"So it is."

"*And* freezing."

"Is it?"

"Yes," said Eeyore. "However," he said, brightening up a little, "we haven't had an earthquake lately." *The House At Pooh Corner*

Remember that many people prefer talking
to those who discuss Sensible Things and use short,
easy words, like "What about lunch?"

———⬦⬦⬦———

When making conversation, be sure to speak in a
manner that the listener will understand.

———⬦⬦⬦———

"The atmospheric conditions have been very unfavourable lately," said Owl.

"The what?"

"It has been raining," explained Owl.

"Yes," said Christopher Robin. "It has."

"The flood-level has reached an unprecedented height."

"The who?"

"There's a lot of water about," explained Owl.

Winnie-the-Pooh

The family is a popular topic of conversation, but remember that it is only likely to interest one's closest friends-and-relations.

In general, keep in mind that a subject fascinating to you may not always fascinate others.

Roo was washing his face and paws in the stream, while Kanga explained to everybody proudly that this was the first time he had ever washed his face himself, and Owl was telling Kanga an Interesting Anecdote full of long words like Encyclopaedia and Rhododendron to which Kanga wasn't listening.

Winnie-the-Pooh

*T*alking at length about a topic that bores the listener is not only impolite but sometimes dangerous.

Owl told him a very long story about an aunt who had once laid a seagull's egg by mistake, and the story went on and on, rather like this sentence, until Piglet who was listening out of his

window without much hope, went to sleep quietly and naturally, slipping slowly out of the window towards the water until he was only hanging on by his toes, at which moment luckily, a sudden loud squawk from Owl, which was really part of the story, being what his aunt said, woke the Piglet up and just gave him time to jerk himself back into safety and say, "How interesting, and did she?"

Winnie-the-Pooh

When face-to-face with a Heffalump, it is
best not to make conversation at all. When it says,
"Ho-ho!" just hum to yourself.

———❦———

Remember that not everyone is willing or able
to make light conversation or small talk.

———❦———

"Good morning, Eeyore," said Pooh.

"Good morning, Pooh Bear," said Eeyore gloomily. "If it *is* a good morning," he said. "Which I doubt," said he.

Winnie-the-Pooh

A good conversationalist knows that small talk, though pleasant, is no substitute for more meaningful discussion.

"Not conversing," said Eeyore. "No Give and Take. No Exchange of Thought: 'Hallo——What'—I mean, it gets you nowhere, particularly if the other person's tail is only just in sight for the second half of the conversation."

The House At Pooh Corner

Fortunately, with your best friends, it is unnecessary to be concerned about making conversation. With them, you can feel comfortable talking about anything—or nothing.

They began to talk in a friendly way about this and that, and Piglet said, "If you see what I mean, Pooh," and Pooh said, "It's just what I think myself, Piglet," and Piglet said, "But, on the other hand, Pooh, we must remember," and Pooh said, "Quite true, Piglet, although I had forgotten it for the moment."

Winnie-the-Pooh

❧ Correspondence ❧

*There are some who feel that written correspondence
is unnecessary and a Bother.*

Eeyore was saying to himself, "This writing business. Pencils and what-not. Over-rated, if you ask me. Silly stuff. Nothing in it."

Winnie-the-Pooh

———— ∞ ————

*In the Hundred Acre Wood and elsewhere,
those who know how to write a proper letter are much
respected and in great demand.*

———— ∞ ————

So Owl wrote…and this is what he wrote:

HIPY PAPY BTHUTHDTH THUTHDA BTHUTHDY.

Pooh looked on admiringly.

"I'm just saying 'A Happy Birthday,'" said Owl carelessly.

"It's a nice long one," said Pooh, very much impressed by it.

Winnie-the-Pooh

If you must step out while expecting visitors,
it is a wise and thoughtful idea to write a note for your
door saying that you have Gon Out and are Bisy
but will be Backson.

A letter is a good way to communicate
important information. If the matter is urgent, you
should follow up in person later.

Pooh had had a Mysterious Missage underneath his front door that morning, saying, "I AM SCERCHING FOR A NEW HOUSE FOR OWL SO HAD YOU RABBIT," and while he was wondering what it meant, Rabbit had come in and read it for him.

"I'm leaving one for all the others," said Rabbit, "and telling them what it means." *The House At Pooh Corner*

---

*K*eep a bottle handy so that you can send a letter in the
event that you are ever Surrounded by Water.

---

*R*emember that letter writing is more than
an important social skill; it could also save your life.

At last he found a pencil and a small piece of dry paper, and a bottle with a cork to it. And he wrote on one side of the paper:

HELP!

PIGLET (ME)

and on the other side:

IT'S ME PIGLET, HELP HELP.

Winnie-the-Pooh

Be sure to write all correspondence neatly and clearly. Otherwise, the recipient may need the help of a Clever Reader to figure it out.

Whether it's a simple Missage or an important Rissolution, always check what you have written for mistakes. Rewrite it if necessary; a perfectly written letter will reflect well on you.

Rabbit brained out a Notice, and this is what it said:

"Notice a meeting of everybody will meet at the House at Pooh Corner to pass a Rissolution By Order Keep to the Left Signed Rabbit."

He had to write this out two or three times before he could get the rissolution to look like what he thought it was going to when he began to spell it. *The House At Pooh Corner*

Consider developing your own distinctive signature. Though not necessary, it is a nice way to give your correspondence a little personal style.

𝒸𝑜𝑅

Piglet

Kanga

Rabbit

Other Useful Etiquette Tips

"Thank you" is the proper thing to say when you
have been made a Knight.

You should also say "Thank you" after
receiving applause—even if it is a bit late in coming.

"If anybody wants to clap," said Eeyore when he had read this, "now is the time to do it."

They all clapped.

"Thank you," said Eeyore. "Unexpected and gratifying, if a little lacking in Smack." *The House At Pooh Corner*

It is perfectly acceptable to have a Proper Tea following a Very Nearly tea, which is one you forget about afterwards.

Using words like "please" and "could you very sweetly" is not just good etiquette; it is good sense. After all, polite requests are most likely to be granted.

"Do you think you could very kindly lean against me, 'cos I keep pulling so hard that I fall over backwards."

Pooh sat down, dug his feet into the ground, and pushed hard against Christopher Robin's back, and Christopher Robin pushed hard against his, and pulled and pulled at his boot until he had got it on.   *Winnie-the-Pooh*

---※---

Remember to cover your mouth when you cough, or you may accidentally bounce someone into the river.

---※---

*If you hurt someone's feelings—
or any other part—be sure to apologize.*

---※---

You aimed very carefully at the balloon, and fired.

"*Ow!*" said Pooh.

"Did I miss?" you asked.

"You didn't exactly *miss*," said Pooh, "but you missed the *balloon*."

"I'm so sorry," you said, and you fired again, and this time you hit the balloon, and Winnie-the-Pooh floated down to the ground.

Winnie-the-Pooh

It is proper to wish someone celebrating a birthday many happy returns of the day. A gift, such as a Very Useful Pot that used to contain honey, is usually not necessary but very nice nonetheless.

It is really not proper to invite yourself along on an Expotition. But if you do so, bring your own Provisions— and try to keep out of everyone else's way.

First came Christopher Robin and Rabbit, then Piglet and Pooh; then Kanga, with Roo in her pocket, and Owl; then Eeyore; and, at the end, in a long line, all Rabbit's friends-and-relations.

"I didn't ask them," explained Rabbit carelessly. "They just came. They always do. They can march at the end, after Eeyore."

Winnie-the-Pooh

The key to good etiquette is remembering that a little Consideration, a little Thought for Others, makes all the difference.